New Horizons

by Brian A. Couture
& Donald F. Goodwin, Jr.

New Horizons
Copyright © 2019 by Brian A. Couture and Donald
F. Goodwin, Jr.

Published by Piscataqua Press
an imprint of RiverRun Bookstore
32 Daniel Street
Portsmouth NH 03801

ISBN: 978-1-950381-17-3

About the Author

I was brought up going to church and attended Roman Catholic religion classes. I have traveled the world as a young U.S.M.C. soldier in military service of my country. I have come to believe three persons in one divine God are my strength.

Jesus the immaculate savior is my shield,
Stories of the Holy Bible are my horse,
God's words are my sword.

May health of mind and body,
Peace of heart and soul, mind clarity,
A strong, healthy belief in all-mighty God
Be with you forever.

PEACE,

Sincerely,
Brian A. Couture

I have loved animals, domestic and wild, for as long as I can remember. I have brought and cared for hurt and sick animals to the veterinarians and the S.P.C.A., both me and my father would volunteer to walk dogs and spend time with other animals.

My favorite wild animal is the American wolf. I admire their natural beauty and their ability to survive in the wild. I have cared for and raised rabbits, guineas, rats, and birds. I have and do as I said – admire wild animals from a distance in their natural habitats.

I have especially enjoyed time shared with my grandfather and uncles. I like walking Clyde and watching him make new friends, human and animal.

Peace to you and your family,
Donald F. Goodwin, Jr.

For Andrea

The person who made it possible for me to get this book published - her selfless efforts and do or die attitude helped her to persevere over problems and help me to be a published author.

A thousand thanks, Andrea.

Brian A. Couture
Donald F. Goodwin, Jr.

PART I

Coming into Summer

I

Everything is waking up.
In spring, the vastness erupts.
Slowly rising up we see
The snow is gone now
The grass is growing green
Plants are pushing up from the fertile soil
Soon the flowers will bloom
We will pick them to brighten our homes

II

The days are getting longer now
Summertime is here
Warmer weather
We waited so long
Through the winter storms
All gone.

To Authority Figures

You can bind my hands and feet in steel shackles
     and chains
Close up my eyes, shut up my mouth and lock me in a
     cold, dark, damp closet.
Yet after all of this I shall still remain free
For my soul soars in the Heavens and my mind resides with
     all-mighty God.

Winter Dawn

The sun half risen
Creating a wonderful light,
Through the clean, crisp, late winter air
The ice covered snow glistens
Reflecting the morning's light
Enriching my mood
To a brilliant new height.

NATURE

The air is clean
With a full sweetness
Of spring's new life
The late days damp, warm, kisses intently
Invite themselves to ourselves
Awakening our most inner spirit
To one of God's most beautiful creations
Mother Nature herself
As we walk along
Our sense intake reveals
Sheer, breathtaking beauty
Hazy, blue-pink sky
Meets lush green forest
Meeting rich Mother Earth
As she provides nourishment
For flower, fish, plant and mammal.

The Park Bench

I came here
A long time ago
I guess maybe a couple of years or so
I like this place I found.
It is a nice, quiet, country bench
Near a river
I watched back then
A muskrat building its den
Probably getting ready, for babies, I guess
It was fun watching it toil away the day
It was nice and cool there too
There was a stand of trees
Blocking the direct sunlight
A cooling effect the trees have
On this area of grass,
I never see anyone there though
They are missing out on so much
This little hideaway
It is God's own touch
I guess in a way
It is a blessing
That I found this place, that day.

MOTHER NATURE'S SOUND

I hear it in the whistle of the wind as it passes through the
    branches of the trees.
I hear it in the waves of the ocean, as the waves crash against
    the rocks on a sea breeze.
I hear it in the songs of the birds as they awaken to
    greet the morning.
I hear it in the talking and laughing of people as
    they wile away the hours of the day.
I hear it in the gurgle of a stream, as it flows past.
I hear it in the splash of a speckled trout as it rises up
    for a fly.
I hear it in the breathing and heartbeat of my lover,
    as we lie close together.
I hear it in the music I listen to, passing the time of day.
I hear it in the voice of priests saying their Sunday sermons.
I hear it in the sounds of nature as I spend time
    in the Great North Woods.
I hear it in many sounds, as I live my life.
I just know I will continue to hear God's voice
    as long as I can hear Mother Nature's sound.

FLY HIGH

Eagle you fly
On the breeze
Over the rocky
Mountain peaks.
You feed your young
Fresh animal flesh
Regurgitated bounty
From the hunt
In which you excel
A cunning adversary
Of most small game
You soar in flight
Proud and strong
You are a told messenger
Between man and God
Bringing our prayers to the Heavens
Eagle you fly
On the breeze
Over the rocky
Mountain peaks

Trains of Yesterday

I really don't want to go anywhere
I would like to stay here in my chair
Sometimes that ramblin' feelin' just hits me
I want to go,
Where the whistles blow
From locomotive's gone now
That feelin' just hits my heart
Where the steam engines don't blow
Their whistles anymore
People don't go on a ramble,
Like they used to
Hobos riding the boxcars
To places often unknown
Amusing themselves with whiskey and wine,
Bringing musical instruments of all kinds
Spinning yarns and singing songs
They just didn't know
Their hearts would long
For the sound of that old whistle blowin'
On trains of yesterday.

THE TREE
VERSION I

A mixture of leaf-covered branches

Entangled, entwined

Reaching for the sky

And Heavens far beyond

Big to small, smaller to leaf

With sunlight shining through,

The branches and leaves of the tree

The streams of light filtering down to the ground

Clear blue sky

Way up high

With God looking down at me,

Looking at this tree I see

It looks like it belongs in Africa to me

I guess it just grows there

Branches entangled

Reaching for the sky

A wonder to anyone's open eyes.

Cynthia I

She was the lighthouse
Against the storm
Shining her light
Bright, clam and warm
She was a palm
For all to hold on to
She was the shelter,
That kept out the wind and rain
She brightened the halls,
The corridors of gloom
She was a voice that said
Come to me
I will shelter you
From all harmful seas.

Cynthia II

She was in my dream
It was really nice
I guess I liked her
More than I realized
When I was with her
Because my brain keeps conjuring her up
In my mind
She is in my night and daydreams
I hope she fares well
Wherever she is
She was just one more gift
That I missed.

Up and Down the Street

She walks up and down the street
Looking for ways to something
Hardly ever there
She strives for that everyday
Circumstances beyond her control
Will not allow her that
Even though her desire
eats her soul
She probably started young –
Maybe on the trails, on the way to school
Or maybe it was involved in a romantic interlude
With a boy she liked in school.
She chases that feeling
Once experienced (by some people)
Might never be found again
Maybe it was her first shot of whiskey
Just let it trickle down her throat,
Oh that warm feeling in her body
I guess just relief from that dry, scratchy throat.
That it would seem only alcohol could quench
It never really does for long anyway
Possibly it quelled the urge for a while
Yet it never really quells the thirst for long

ODE TO HELEN G.

She died there
On an old dirt road
Her old body just collapsed
Could not take it anymore

Just another day
On the search
For John Barelycorn

A PRAYER AND A WISH

For Helen G.

Father give her
An old-fashioned bar
Some place warm
Some place nice
Pleasant to her
Her outlook on life
Show her a big
Neon sign
Beer and eats
A place where she can go
To do some twelve-ounce curls
Or to sedate the memories
Just let it all go
A place where the beer
Flows and flows

WE'LL GATHER THERE

I'm going down
To the railway station
Riding the rails
People of all nations
Let's gather there
Boarding the train
All of God's children
Riding the rails
Through time and space
Soon arriving at Heaven's gate –
God is the engineer
Piloting this train
He will take us all
Through time and space
Soon we will arrive
At Heaven's gate

Mother Nature's Dress

She wears a dress
Made up of all the treasures of nature
Her dress is of flowers and trees, all of God's creatures
She wears them so well
Dresses according to the season
Spring and summer, fall and winter
She wears them all
It is wonderful to see them.

The Long Run in the Night

His teeth sharp

His senses keen

His nose twitches and tingles

From the bite of the cold, winter air. –

He lets out a howl

In a fiery fury, for itself and its pack

Adrenaline flowing

They can't stand still

For food they will hunt

On the long run

In the cold winter night

THE TREE
VERSION II

Clear blue sky

Way up high

Even up to the Heavens

As God looked down at me

Looking at this tree I see

Seems like it belongs in Africa somewhere

I guess it just happened to grow there

Branches entangled

Reaching for the sky

Sun shining down through the branches of leaves

It looks like something

Birds would like to live in

Plenty of branches

For them to play and nest in.

Limitless Beyond and Endless Time

You travel so fast and free
Into the limitless beyond
Fly through the sky
With a watchful eye
Searching the ground
For game to be found
A hunter to feed its young
Its strongest need
To carry on its kind
Into endless time.

How Precious These Gifts

In this tree
A bird I hear
Singing its heavenly song. –
What more precious gift
Could God give to me?
This bird singing here, in the morning
As the sun slowly rises up
The colors I see
More gifts,
Bestowed upon me
Gifts from God
So many more
To hear and see.

Along His Holy Way

There is a statue
Of a Chinese priest
Standing barefoot
On a bed of crushed stone
On a table in my room
His garments hanging, from his shoulders, down past his ankles
His hair mostly made up on top, with hair cascading down
Over his ears, then down past his shoulders
A man of stature it would seem
Probably a priest from some ancient Holy order
Who made a science of self-control
He wears a kind of bead with an ornament hanging from it
Its meaning unknown to me, like most people probably
The cap of the small jar he is sprinkling out, in front of him
Has some type of beads hanging from it and must hold some
Ancient Holy water, like some spiritual tool
A way of warding off evil spirits
As he goes along his Holy way

Salvation

Jesus is coming
On one special day
He will guide us along
In his own special way
We pray forgiveness
We long for your words. –
Come follow my footsteps
I will guide you this day
To my father's home in Heaven
He provides for us in every way
So come on everybody
Sing with us today
Praise God our creator
We love you always.

FRIENDS

As I sit on the beach, as the sun peaks over the horizon
I know I am blessed to have them as friends.
I know that I don't deserve them. Yet they lifted
Me up, and took me into their hearts, like no
One has ever done before, for them I am truly grateful.

As I have heard it said that some people go to
The barren lands to find themselves and God
Somewhere there.
I think that a person, in order to find themselves,
Should go to the city and bring the lord with them,
And these people bring me there.
They crack open my shell and open me up to people and
They bring me, wholeheartedly when we are down
We prop one another back up to face the world again.
I am inspired by them and their inner beauty, as the
Sun is inspired by the seashore to rise slowly up
On the horizon greeting the world with its
Wonderful warmth and light.
When they greet me from time to time, they like
The sunshine, always brighten my day.

It Took the Place

Somehow, somewhere
It took the place of penny candy
It took the place of ice cream
It took the place of my attitude toward it
It took the place of a nice cold or hot soft drink
It took everything over, that's what it did
It took over who I hung around with
It took over who would hang around with me
It took away relationships, feelings, hopes and dreams
Someone once told me there are very powerful
       removers we deal with every day and be careful of.
They remove mothers, fathers, family members,
       friends, cars, motorcycles, houses, and even
       your life.

Active addiction to cigarettes, alcohol and drugs
       is playing with the deadliest removers
       of all. One thing is sure, active addiction
       leads to one of three things

Mental institutions, prisons or death.

A Roadmap of Age

When I looked at him
I could see in his eyes
He was looking back
With amazement in his smile
For what he saw in my face
Was a road map of age
He said thanks for coming
As he looked back in dismay
He knew where he had been
He walked the same path
It was a map of drugs and alcohol
All the trips he had made
In bars and just about anywhere
He shook my hand, and said goodbye
Thanks for showing up
I hope we meet again
We will be on a better path
I need to achieve sobriety
Or the only road ahead
I will be dead.

WHISKEY

I did not have that shot of whiskey

Because I did not buy that bottle of whiskey

I might have just sipped it

Let the warmth roll down my throat

Most probably though, I would have gulped and guzzled it.

My greatest fear is not being able to remember

I did not get that drink of whiskey

Because of course you know

It never ends there anyhow

To be honest, I don't ever remember having one drink.

Yet from time to time

I have entertained the thought of having one drink

I cannot have one drink I know

I have never been able to have one drink

That is why I did not buy that bottle of whiskey today.

SOBRIETY

I hope in time
With help from someone kind
My body will develop
My light will shine
I lived in the past
Mostly alone
I strayed from God's path
The sins of my mortal life
May not be condoned
I woke one morning
A short time ago
My life is worth more than a pot or drink high
I pray in the future
With memories of the past
With a devout will, and strong body
My sobriety will last.

DEATH'S BED

As I lay

On my back

In my bed

My oh so permanent death's bed

The end so near or God forbid so dreadfully far away

Time passes each second like a day

I find myself praying for the end to come

Yet I have been, in this, my death's bed for more than a
      year now, or is it ten thousand years

My mind wanders and strays

Back and forth

In and out

Near and far

Past to present

People come in and go out

Chatting and laughing and rustling about

Sisters and nieces and nephews come out

To visit me and often they have to shout

So that I know what they are talking about

Often I don't want visitors to come to see me in
      the condition I am in.

I wish they would stay away

Remember me the way I was in my youth

Some special time in my life
Rather than come see me now
I think, just look at me
My hair is white
My body is shriveled and joints bent
My skin is sagging and wrinkled
My eyes have sunken into my head
What a monstrous scheme to put me on display
Here, in this, my death's bed
I have not moved my body of my own volition
            in many months now
I must be fed
I must be diapered
I must be washed and groomed
Should I have a choice in the matter
Yesterday would have been too long a wait
For me to pass away
Then walk to Heaven's gate

The Light in Death

As I walk through a field of straw and wildflowers,
> The smell that comes to my nose is so sweet

I reach the edge of the field and enter a hardwood forest,
> The leaves rustle under my feet as I walk along

I walk a bit farther and notice the beautiful beams of
> Sunlight, shining through the leaves and branches of
> trees

I walk farther still, then sit with my back against a
> Big maple tree

I notice the beams of sunlight again and wander about
> The light

Through my life I have always thought that light is good and
> Spiritual light is brightest

I have heard that bright light in dreams and in death
> We should always follow, the reason being
> That it is movement toward the good. I have
> Thought that each day we are alive we move closer
> To death.

In dying though, we do not reach an end, we come
> To a new beginning.

We move to a circle of life, of existence, so good
> And beautiful that it would boggle the human mind.

PEACE OF MIND AND BODY

Peace at heart of mind and body
Tranquility, infinitely in waves of blue
Flowing through my mind
To travel timelessly and effortlessly
My spirit of course
Somewhere within me
My mortal mind seeks and makes progress daily
After having sought for so long
The fear at inevitable, long fight against
Unacceptable death dissipates with age
And each life situation I go through

Visions

As I sit here quietly alone
I experience things
I did not know
Had never been shown
For God above is the master of the plan
He shows me things from time to time
The visions he shows me, the beauty of nature
With animals and spirits all around
In this nature vision, I see, before me
It could only be God, who else could it be
Eagles flying in canyons around
Black bears roaming, deer feeding contentedly
The things I see are very beautiful
The call of nature tugging at my soul
Calling me to the woods
Like it has done so often
Making me a more full and complete person

The Great Wankin Tonka

As he stands before, then bends and kneels, to drink from
>The clear cool pond,

He notices the reflections of himself and the beautiful
>Blue sky and white puffy clouds

As water settles, he sees, more clearly the reflections

He notices the Autumn leaves changing to their brilliant colors

He looks at his own reflection, and sees his suntanned skin,
>The adornment of colors of paint on his face and arms

He sees his pants, boots and shirt made of softened deer
>Hide and his knife and hatchet made of bone,

>Stone and raw hide

He looks up at the Heavens and outstretches his arms
>As if to hug someone and says

I am sixteen years old today, I have been on a
>Journey, to find myself and my mission in life

Keeping his position and closing his mouth, as if to
>Have spoken to God and waiting for a response

He hears a shriek and sees an eagle flying over
>The pond

The eagle dives for the water and catches a fish

It flies to a cliff and deposits the fish into its
>Nearby nest of chicks

The eagle flies over the pond, once more, screeches,
>Flies past the pond and catches a rabbit

The eagle flies back to its nest.

The boy bows and thanks God and says

I have my mission in life, for to fish and hunt

      To support my people is a very honorable

      Mission.

Manitoba

As you are a constellation of stars
I gaze up at all your majesty
Then everything becomes prismatic
The stars begin to move and form a bear
The bear levitates to the ground and stand upright
> On its back legs,
He lets out a growl and goes from an upright
> Position to stand on all four peaceful paws
In all his majesty he breaks into a run and
> Crashes into a nearby river, with the
> Power of the Gods
I see you fish there, your rewards, a salmon
> You took from the currents of the river
You proudly saunter away from the river,
> Stand up on your back legs and levitate
> Up to the Heavens with the constellations
> Of stars.

REFLECTIONS

Water falling from the mountaintop
Into a pool full of trout
The sand on the edge of the pool is warm on my
Bare feet
The sun shining on the falls, make the
Drops of water shine like diamonds
The trees around the falls turn to their
Autumn colors of red, yellow and orange
The reflections of the trees and leaves on
The pool are pretty, as the ripples mix
The fall colors into a magnificent
Sight.

Only You

Today when you woke
Blindly walking into the living room
I looked at you and fell in love all over again
Today when I compare my life, with any other
        Time in my life
Nothing compares to today with you
I really feel good about myself
You found me in the bottom of a bottle of
        Whiskey
Then unconditionally loved and brought me
        Back to good health
For that I am truly grateful
Thank you for loving me the way you do

I Always Miss You (When You Are Away)

As we stand hand in hand
Watching the sun set
The sky full of yellow, orange, pink and blue
All I want to tell you is that I love you
It just seems too little
Then we turn and kiss
That makes me realize
How much I would have missed
Had I not met you
Yet time goes on
The sunset lingers on
While time passes so pleasantly,
Whenever I am with you
I hope just the time we spend together
Shows you how much I do love you
When we are apart
I always miss you.

You Asked Me To Write You A Poem

You asked me to write you a poem
I write poetry from time to time
To write a poem to say how I feel about you
Gee! I don't know if I can find the words
Just to tell you how much gratitude I have for
      Having you in my life
You have been there for me no matter what
I feel though, if you ever left I would simply
      Cease to exist.
You are nourishment for my soul
You sustain me, and the time we have had
      Together, no other time in my life could
      compare
You make me feel whole, you make me feel alive
      Again, for a long time I think I was dead
Just the sound of your voice causes my soul to
      Leap with joy.
I have never been happier than being with you has
      Left me
We have been together for a long time now
I thank God you have had the patience to put
      Up with me
I love you with all my heart
The thought of being without you greatly saddens me

If I had a wish it would simply be to live
    The rest of my life with you
I know though, deep in my heart, I don't need
        To wish for you to spend the rest of your life
        With me
The things you say to me and the way you touch
        Me gives me great confidence that
        We will be together for the rest of our lives
I love you with all my heart
I wish you all the happiness in the world
I hope that just being with me brings you that
        Peace and happiness always
I believe I will love you always and forever
If I could I would build you a stairway to the stars
So that you could climb on every step
I know that once you get to the top you would
        Shine as brightly as the stars above
I know that is where you belong for people to
        Gaze up at
You are so beautiful that you would give
        Anyone a sense of peace
For they would know that God exists,
        Because it would take all mighty God
        To create someone as beautiful as you.

SHARING OUR LOVE TOGETHER

Everything I want to do for you with my love
You do for me with yours
I feel comfortable enough around you to have conversations
Through the day, at night you make me feel happy to be
With you
When we have to part, you make me feel safe with the
Security that you will be back soon
When you return, we laugh and play like two people
In love do
You make me want to give you the sun and
Stars and moon
You at times make me feel helpless, and
Then at times stronger than I have ever
Felt before
I feel as though I can't be without you in
My life
I love you with all my heart
My never-ending desire
Is to always be with you.

Puppy Love

I love her
But she doesn't know
For I am too shy
To tell her
We were just
Two kids in school
I noticed her there
At her desk
In her chair
She seemed
So devoted
To the teacher
But I did not care
I tried to get her
To notice me there
We were just
Two kids in school
In a classroom
We shared
But I guess,
Another
Had caught
Her eye

I was just

Too shy

To tell her

How I felt

Just that I care

She went to the school dance

With her newfound friend

I danced with another

She was very nice and pretty

She seemed to like me

After a few dances

I fell in love

All over again

With the girl I was dancing with

I was so glad

The first did not work out

For the second made me happy

For I felt I was really

With a girl who loved me

Someone I knew

Could make me happy.

The Colors You Bring

The colors in my mind
Are the colors of the rainbow
They are there because of you
I know that because before you
The only colors that were there
Were shades of gray
I guess not very pretty,
To look at,
As the colors of you
Now the colors,
Are all of the rainbow
Red and green, yellow and blue
I know I don't have to wait very long,
For a summer shower
To see a rainbow of color
All I have to do
Is take a look at you.

Talking to God

I met a man
Somewhere in my lifetime
I love him, I think he is so beautiful
Do you love him?
I'll bet he loves you
I meet him in secret, sometimes at home,
Or in the car, or just about anywhere
Hmmm
Psst
This beautiful man just visits to sit and talk to me
Do you know what
All I have to do to get him to visit is put my
Hands together and pray
Simply say Father I am troubled today or
Maybe, Father I thought I would call you
To tell you I am so happy today and
Lord Jesus I love you.

PASTELS

We are moving right along now
Keeping our minds and bodies clean
We are building a special place
A home, or maybe even a castle
Shining and beautiful with the light of life
Only with proper eating habits and hygiene practices
A good positive attitude and a few prayers
At night before we sleep and in the morning
When we wake
We say the Lord's Prayer, a Hail Mary, and Glory Be
We ask blessings for our loved ones and pets
The more diligent we are in our worship
Of our Lord and God
The sooner and more brilliantly we will see
It gleam.

I Endure Still

The expectations of the world that surrounds me
Compel my emotions to sense
A realization that grows within me
To explore the realities of life, love and moral growth
Yet some power within me
Will not let the reins free
To allow my will to endure too easily
Yet I will not allow self-defeat
These forces within me
Battle on daily
Project an impression of being too weak
But with a positive attitude
I do believe
It is God's will
I endure still.

God is Everywhere

God is everywhere
So come and say a special prayer
For those who sometimes fear
They may have strayed from his son's care
God is everywhere
So come and show you care
Let's say a simple prayer
For those who may have strayed somewhere
God is everywhere
He knows we care
Because we lead them here
Back to Jesus flock with care
God is everywhere
We can teach them here
Jesus will always care
So say his father's prayer
God is everywhere
His son will lead us back with care
Just kneel and say a special prayer
To God who is always there
God is everywhere
We must show God by the way we treat one another
No matter what happens in mortal life
Treat with respect acquaintances, friends and family

Everyone is hopefully striving for the same thing
A place in Heaven with our Lord the king.

GIVING CHRIST HIS DUE

When Jesus is born in our hearts
Heaven is revealed in our minds
Our souls are challenged with the difference
Between right and wrong
With help from our guardian angel
Who is guided by God to help us make decisions
That will decide our fate
These decisions will show God the purity of our heart and soul
God created us all equal to one another
No one is a superior being except God
God is all mighty and [all love] for his children
When I have troubles, I look to my heart and
Pray to Jesus for answers for my troubles
And problems
Our heart is where Jesus lives
Of late I pray for understanding of why certain
People try to control me
I have done very little wrong in many years
I don't' want you to get me wrong. I sin
As every human sins
I pray for the grace from Jesus so that I can
Control the rage in my soul for my life's
Losses and gains, no matter how small
Or great they may be

I love Jesus with all my heart, mind, soul and strength
I try never to let him down
When I make a mistake I pray to God for
My heart felt sorrow for my transgressions
When I do this, I feel peace in my heart and
Soul and feel humbled
I do and feel this because of my compunction
For Jesus Christ.

PART II

Heart + Soul

As long as he could remember
He wanted to be a mountain man
So he fished and trapped and hunted his way
Deeper into the mountains everyday
He never again had a yearning for the lower lands
It was like he wanted the mountains and her bounty
For so long and so intensely
Mother nature took him
Heart and soul
So he wandered
In search of his possessions
Never to leave the mountains again
Of his own free will.
So he made it
It would seem
Through life here on Earth
Past his death
Yet he walked along
To find the gates of Heaven
But he was so tired from the ordeal
When all of a sudden
God lowered his hand
Like a cushiony, cottony bed of clouds
So the man accepted it

He rested there
On his way to Heaven

Just For Snoopy

Snooper, you darling, deary, black dog
You brighten my days and make the long
Winter nights shorter
You kiss my face when I climb into bed
You are a treasure to have and a wonder to hold
You howl to the music on the radio
You bring my spirit to a brilliant new height
I love to watch you in the backyard
It makes me happy to see you play
Swimming in the pond with White Fang was fun
Your brother had to go, we miss him so
I am sure you must miss him too
He was a wonderful companion like you
We will not part til you have to go to Heaven
I will miss you more than you know
I will [pontificate] about you fondly
Maybe howling to the music on the radio. –

RIP "Poop"
December 21, 2012

Congenial Hearts

He loved her spirit
She was a one of a kind, wonderous form
A spirit warm and delightful
People would gather
To experience her strength
When she spoke of life and love
Now he was tall and handsome
Stately, kind of
Like most of all wild creatures are stately
It is just that sense they project
Because they are wild and free
He was kind of like a soft falling snow in October
When it is still not too cold
The big flakes, the kind you like to catch on your tongue
Just to savor the flavor
He was a presence calm and delightful
She met him there, in spirit of course, far
Beyond their time
Like some intergalactic spirits would if they could
Interact in some Heavenly way.

WILLIE (THE MOUSE) WILLIMINEO

If I could get into her cage
But I just won't fit
How happy we would be
Friends for her lifetime
I would just
Caress her coat
To let her know
What good friends
We could be
She toils all day
Playing,
Eating her seeds away
Willie my good friend
You are a Godsend

I Love the Effect She Has On Me

Her effect on me was like that, of a subtle warmth, slowly
Washing over my body, caressing my skin, moving my
Soul to a state of sheer bliss
Then she touched my shoulder, to get me to come around
Again, when another warmth started in, to reinforce
The first warmth, like strength throughout my whole body
She spoke to me, the sounds coming from her throat
Were as peaceful and soothing as the singing
And chirping of small birds on a cool spring morning
Looking at her face, at different times of the day,
Puts a glow in my heart and gives me
Purpose and meaning.

TRACES OF SNOOPY

Traces of Snoopy are all around
The scents Clyde smells are in every room
On his blanket, in his bed
Clyde just lays there
He just doesn't understand Snoopy is dead
We tell him Snoopy went home to Heaven
But he still smells traces of him all around
He doesn't understand why he is no where
To be found

The Galaxy Orb

The galaxies are all in place

Some going somewhere

Others going elsewhere

Never to know

Where it has been

Or

Where it will go

But is it all

In a little plastic bell

On the belt of someone

No one can remember

Because so many galaxies have come and gone

So he wades into the river

Behind his cabin

With his wader boots and fly rod in hand

He's looking for the big lunkers

Waiting in the pools

To feed somewhere there

I will bet he wishes it could be on command

They only bite when the moon is just right

He loosens the strap on the pouch on his side

Up in his hand is the super galaxy orb beside

So he blows a whisper of breath on the orb

That is all it takes from him

The super universe is set in motion again
All the stars and planets adjust
He sets the orb back in its pouch
He notices the stars look brighter
Maybe it will be a good night
He feels more comfortable
He casts another fly
A fish strikes
He sets the hook and reels it in
A nice native speckled trout
He slides the fish into his creele
I guess maybe that is what's real
A brookie for supper
Oh boy what a meal.

SPRINGS

Walking along
I hear and see
Birds singing their songs
So harmoniously,
Piercing through the warm, damp summer air
Animals of all kinds gather here
The fresh water spring
Provides for them all
It brings bugs
For birds and small animals to eat
It brings soft water plants
For the vegetarians among them
Plenty of meat for other animals to eat.

Hunting Party
Part I

I sit cross-legged

The fire roaring

With plenty of wood aside

To add more fuel

To stoke it up high

Sparks a flying

I feel the warmth

On my body and face

The rest of the bend

Sitting and standing around the heat

Looking at the fire

Lingering conversations

Of past hunts and weeks

They are getting excited

Ready for the hunt tonight

Bows and arrows

Spears and knives

Honed into sharp tools of the trade

For a successful hunt

The medicine man prayed

Hunting Party
Part II

The scouts are back

There is a black bear, not far away

The medicine man conveys the message

To the rest of the band

They are excited

Projecting ahead

Just in the woods

They form a line

Walking in the direction

The scouts said the bear would be

They get closer

They can hear the heavy breathing

Its there, in the brush

They start to bring the line

To a circle

The bear is surrounded

He growls a mournful cry,

HUNTING PARTY
PART III

The bear rears on its back legs

A mistake on his part

Someone darts in with a spear, stabs the bear

And runs

Arrows strike the bear

He is screeching and growling and crying

They continue the attack

The bear drops to the ground

Breathing loudly and moaning

The bear quickly dies

The members of the band

Are yelling and crying out in victory

It was a good hunt

The band thanks God for hearing the

Medicine man's prayers.

A Meeting Place

Not to be the student or the teacher

Not to be the aggressor or the aggressee

A state of being, not to be the affected or the affectee

A state of mind neutral

To be a drop, without making a splash as it

Meets the pond

To allow the drop with no turbulence

As the pond accepts the drop as a familiar

Part of itself, by accepting another form

Of itself, by releasing the uncomfortability

Emanating from the drop

In gentle wave like form moving outward

Away from the meeting point

Of the drop and itself.

In the Breeze

Amber butterflies
Fluttering and floating about
Around the swift river
What a sight
Rugged beauty is everywhere
Near the river itself
It is the lore of the butterflies
In the gentle breeze
What an experience to behold
The sights we see
The sounds we hear
The smells we breathe.

Fly Fishing Heron

The heron plucks a feather
Then drops it into the water
It patiently waits
The fisher with feathers as flies
Then a rise
From a fish
Enticed by the feather
The heron strikes and eats the fish
Then plucks another feather
Drops it into the water
Then patiently waits.

All in a Haze of Grey

Well I am just blessed
With this wonderful sight
There at quite a distance
Walking along
A bit of a kind of eerie view
These two figures
Slowly moving through the woods
A master following his dog
The fog causing the figures
To look like vague shadows
Slowly walking along
All in a damp, foggy haze of grey

THE SWIFT RIVER

The wind blows through the trees
Rustling leaves blow in the breeze
Fly fishers wade into the river
Below the Kancamagus Highway
Elusive trout, rise after flies, cast by fishers
In their fishing garb, vests and waders on their bodies
Fishermen travel from far and wide
To fish the Swift River
It runs from Gunstock to Conway
In the middle of New Hampshire
The river has run there for hundreds of years
To carry a fly from a case
Trying to entice a trout from a pool
Well that is what it is all about
Fly fishing it seems
The Swift River
Surrounded by the White Mountains
I have always thought of it as a fisher's dream.

Robin

Well, I was just sitting on the steps
It was kind of a warm October
When then I spied a robin
Not in a tree, or even on the lawn
It was in a puddle of water
Washing its tiny body
In the front of the house
On the side of the road
I wish a touch
Just caress its small feathery body
As it splashes the water
All over its head and wings
As it grooms itself
While the morning sun beams down
On its back and crown
I guess God was just
Wishing me a good morning
As he goes along
Into a new day.

ANOTHER HUNT

Wolf you wander
Precariously on the hunt tonight
Food is scarce
As the cold north wind blows in winter
You go to a field,
To settle for mice
Under the snow and crusts of ice
The nourishment keeping you strong
Through the long winter months
Just another wolf
On a cold winter hunt.

CREEPY, CRAWLY CREATURE, I SEE

I saw this creature
Swimming on a pond
I wondered where it came from
Where was it going?
I never saw anything like it in my lifetime
It was a beautiful thing to see
This tan creature
Something must have frightened it
For it to travel in the midday heat
Well, it was a really big surprise to me
Some people say they don't exist
I think they are not looking in the right places
It was a timber rattler
One of the most elusive snakes
It was really a remarkable sight
I watched as it swam along
Then it just dove to the bottom of the pond
And was gone.

A Tactical Fishing Hawk

Steam rising from the pond
Blowing around in the soft breeze beyond
Then it came into view
As I scan the surface of the pond
And its surroundings
It is a hawk
Perched on a half-submerged log
Waiting for minnows
Rising to the surface
So it can pluck them from the water
Then a ripple
In the surface of the pond
The hawk strikes in an instant
Catches the fish
Flies out of sight
Wow! He's gone.

Ladybug

Ladybug on my window so near
You bring a joy to my heart so dear
You flutter away on wings in the breeze
My heart content to see you leave
Cause I know on some other unforeseen day
You will come again to make me feel good
Wish you could stay
Really wish you would
I know you have to go
Where the wind blows
I know you will return
Springtime next year
God bless you in your travels today
Thanks for the good feeling
You brought my way

It Passes By Here

The river that flows by here
Well, with such a dry summer
I guess it just seems to be dead
Just into autumn
The leaves are turning gold and orange and red
Seems that way right now though
Just a shower
Then it will flow
Because of the underground springs
Mountain run off
All seems to bring a river of life
Even bringing birds to sing.

The Hawk

It seems, at first, kind of awful
To see such a thing from afar
But I stay there, quietly, for a while, when
To me, on second thought, it was so
Extremely natural.
If I wanted to stop it
I should have second thoughts
To stop this natural occurrence
A hawk from killing its prey that it has grasped
In its claws
It would be like trying to stop a rageful river
One that is full of the mountains' melted snow
One that is free to run in the spring
I could not stop this natural occurrence
A hawk from killing its prey
Who am I to stop this hawk
From doing such a natural thing?

The Mountain

I see a mountain green with trees and grey with rock
A stream coming down from way up on top
I see the sky with white puffy clouds all around
I see eagle and hawks and other beautiful birds,
Flying and perching and singing their songs
I see bears fishing the salmon-filled river
I see muskrats and beavers building their homes
I see white tailed deer and moose grazing on
The grass below the mountain
I see God and Mother Nature toiling away the day.

THE GIFT

I looked and saw, there he was
A vision on the other side of the stream
I looked and saw without a sight
A vision on the other side of the stream and me
I did not look because of the respect in me
The vision became more clear to see
In this vision I experienced of him
He gave me a gift I did not touch for the
Mortal of me
He placed the gift on my fishing vest
I did not touch the gift out of respect for him
Because of this respect
I was allowed to keep the gift for all eternity
The gift a hook
Made out of bone
The greatest gift I have ever known
For I received the gift out of respect
Once he saw my respect for him
I became a friend of his.

Completely Blown Away By Beauty

When I saw your eyes, wider than the ocean and
    deeper and bluer than the sky, I lost
    myself somewhere in them and could not
    be without you for a second longer, for each
    second was like an eternity.
Then I got a sense of your fragrance and it made me
    feel content, as though the Lord gave me a
    cloud to rest on as he stood watch for my
    welfare.
Then I saw the creamy color of your skin, I was
    mesmerized in a state of ecstasy, for the
    color of your skin was warmth to my eyes.
Then I saw the curls of your hair and it was
    plain to me that it was done by angels,
    who had nothing better to do than to create
    a work of art.
Then I saw you walk by; it was as sure a gait
    of perfection as any angel could move.
When I heard your voice, it was as
    though God created a flute for the
    angels in Heaven to play.

Just a Leaf

So delicate as the leaves that tremble
    when the wind blows
So delicate as flowers fragrance
    as it comes to my nose
So beautiful as the sunshine
    that is how she glows
More terrible then a winter storm
    that ugly she can go
I do love her with all my heart
    that I sure do know
For without her I would be a speck
Just a leaf
Among the leaves

Aura of Beauty

This girl exists
As an aura of beauty and softness and power
She has a hold on me like I have never experienced before
This hold is stronger than steel shackles and chains
She has taken my heart and the longer I know her
The more I trust her to keep it
She is so soft and kind, that when I do something
To hurt her, it hurts me too
Sometimes I find myself running around
From place to place, from day to day only
To find peace and comfort when she is
Back in my arms again.

Our Farm

I called you my husband
You called me your wife
So, we were married in a small-town country church
We started our lives
A baby came along
We lived together on a small farm
In the south, it was our life
We loved one another with each passing day
We visited the church in Macon
On Sunday morning where God taught us,
So we learned
We lived on a small farm in Macon raising cattle
That was our life
The baby grew fast as time went on
Before we knew it, he was in high school
Then after college he took his wife
Now they run the farm in Macon
Our son and his wife making a life.

Staying Together

I have always wished for a friend so true
Someone kind and special like you
We have had quite a time together
Doing things we both like to do

A walk in the sunny morning of the day
To watch the doves as they play

I remember standing with you
Watching out the picture window
At the ground covered with early spring frost
Looking for robins to give us a sign
Spring is here and we are still together

Another winter we made it through
I don't know what the future will bring
I do think if we stay together
We will sing along
With the saints in Heaven forever.

Our Whole True Love

Since we have met
I have come to see
You are my one, my only
Whole true love
We take the time
To explore one another's mind
You take me where I long to be
To show our whole true love
Since we take us
Where we both can truly share
Our whole true love
My destination is clear
No matter where we go
As long as we share
Our whole true love
When the day is through
Our destination has remained true
As long as I spend time with you
In our one whole true love.

JANIS

I imagine your breast pressed against mine

Humming softly, your throat making a sound

So soothing to my spirit, I wish we had time

Someday maybe in Heaven we will meet

My greatest wish to plead to God that I would be with you soon

Wishing your lips could touch mine

I have pictures of you, Janis, up on my wall

I look at you all the time

Trying to imagine what it would be like to be in your arms

I can't wait til you come into view

From that point on, I wish we could remain together

Janis, I feel like I love you with all my heart

I know it would be a miracle if we could be together

From that day, it is my hope we will be together for all eternity

I can't wait for your chest to be pressed against mine.

ORB

Luminescent bubble
Floating in the sky
You are so beautiful
You must be a spirit
A Godsend or some entity
From far away
You are bringing me good feelings
That is what you brought me today
A feeling of amazement
Brought forth from the sky
What brought you here?
I have never seen the likes of you
Maybe God wants to thrill me
By setting you afloat
Fly high, spirit being
Back to God with care
Bring God a message
From my heart to his
I love you always
Father, you brought me great cheer.

EARLY MORNING SIGHT

I was just sitting there
When the thought of God occurred to me
So I peeked up at the Heavens
Taking it all in; this blue morning sight
Blue sky with white puffy clouds all around
Then the sight of the light
Th wonderful sun in the sky
Looking so beautiful
That I held that picture
It was a miraculous sight.

GONE ASTRAY

There are some people
Hopefully I pray
Who have simply gone astray
I will try to make a path
To lead them away from Satan's wrath
The path is difficult as we begin
We make amends, do penance for sins
As we go the evil will slow
The path will widen
A light and warmth will begin to grow
As we continue
There really is only one way to go
We say prayer daily now
We read a few verses from the good book
God's words are very important
We must never forget.
We must truly rely on his infinite power and wisdom
To fight the battles, we so often find ourselves in
If you should ever
Find something within you
An empty place
Or something just doesn't seem to fit
Then go ahead, kneel or just sit
Put your hands together and say something like this

Lord, I need your help
I have made plenty of mistakes
I do know now that I need your grace
For without it I have no place
In your home in Heaven
I also think you should try something like this
Say a prayer for someone you love, or haven't
Seen, or just miss
There is one really important thing
I hope you won't forget
God created the world
Then created men
Then gave his son we would not be damned
I hope this will get you on your way
To a place in Heaven
I am sure God will want you to stay.

www.ingramcontent.com/pod-product-compliance
Lightning Source LLC
LaVergne TN
LVHW041232080426
835508LV00011B/1167